SHONEN JUMP GRAPHIC NOVEL

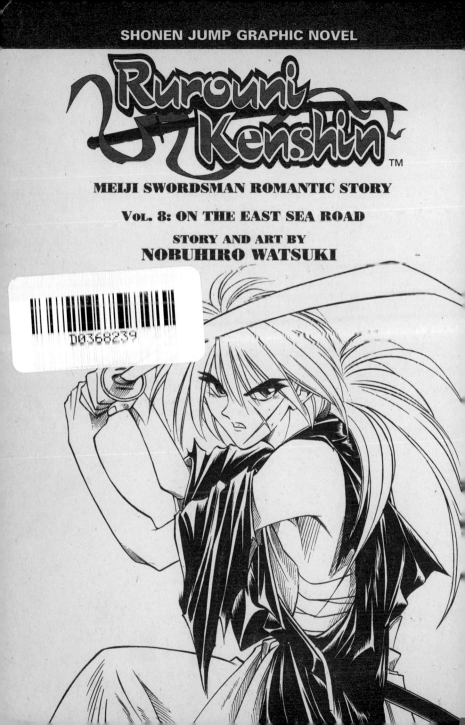


# MEIJI SWORDSMAN ROMANTIC STORY

## Vol. 8: ON THE EAST SEA ROAD

STORY AND ART BY
NOBUHIRO WATSUKI

CAST
緋村剣心（人斬り抜刀斎）
Himura Kenshin (Hitokiri Battōsai)
神谷　薫
Kamiya Kaoru
明神弥彦
Myōjin Yahiko
相楽左之助
Sagara Sanosuke
高荷　恵
Takani Megumi
斎藤　一
Saitō Hajime
巻町　操
Makimachi Misao

A wandering swordsman or *rurouni*, Himura Kenshin carries a *sakabatō*—a sword with an inverted blade—to prevent himself from killing. But, during the civil war that gave birth to the Meiji Era, he inspired awe and terror as the greatest of *hitokiri* as the assassin, Himura Battōsai. After exposing the "false Battōsai" at Kaoru's Kamiya dojo, he remained there to teach swordsmanship. Soon after, he and Kaoru were joined by Myōjin Yahiko, a young man Kenshin saved from the yakuza, and by Sagara Sanosuke, who was inspired by Kenshin to give up the tawdry life of the professional brawler.

Shinomori Aoshi

Seta Sōjirō

# THUS FAR

A man named ***Fujita Gorō*** seriously wounds Sanosuke in combat and challenges Kenshin—at which time he reveals himself to be ***Saitō Hajime***, former officer of the revolutionary Shinsengumi, now a spy sent by the police to test Kenshin's fighting abilities. As ***Shishio Makoto*** (the man who took Kenshin's place as ***hitokiri***) plots against the government, ***Ōkubo Toshimichi*** (famous politician) requests that Kenshin travel to Kyoto and assassinate Shishio Makoto. Kaoru tries to stop him, but when Ōkubo is himself assassinated in broad daylight by one of Shishio's men, Kenshin sets out for Kyoto... saying goodbye only to Kaoru.

# CONTENTS

**RUROUNI KENSHIN**
Meiji Swordsman Romantic Story
BOOK EIGHT: ON THE EAST SEA ROAD

OF ALL THE LOUSY... THAT SELFISH BASTARD!!!

LEAVING WITHOUT SAYING A WORD!!!

C-CALM DOWN!
DON'T MESS UP THE SHOP!
HRR
SCARY!

## Act 58—To Kyoto (Part I)

WELL, THEN, *I'M* GOING TO KYOTO, TOO—
—AND I'M NOT COMING BACK TILL I'VE *BELTED* HIM!!

# Presenting the Results of the 1st "Character Popularity" Contest!!

1st Place:
Himura Kenshin
19,476 Votes

3rd Place:
Myōjin Yahiko
3,659 Votes

5th Place:
Kamiya
Kaoru
2,627
Votes

9th Place:
Takani Megumi
626 Votes

8th Place:
Tsukayama
Yutarō
904 Votes

# (Part 1)

2nd Place:
Sagara Sanosuke
9,991 Votes

6th Place:
Sagara Sōzō
2,157 Votes

7th Place:
Okita Sōshi
1,144 Votes

11th Place:
Saitō Hajime
598 Votes

4th Place:
Shinomori
Aoshi
3,494 Votes

10th Place:
Udō Jin-e
612 Votes

# Act 58—To Kyoto

READ THIS WAY

JUST DON'T YOU GO WANDERING OFF WITHOUT MY SAY-SO!
BLAST HIM!
GONG
HE'S AWFULLY FRUSTRATED ...
YES.
AND... HE DIDN'T PAY AGAIN.

HUH. I NEVER THOUGHT KENSHIN-SAN WOULD GO BACK TO WANDERING.
I REALLY THOUGHT HE'D SETTLE DOWN AT KAORU'S PLACE.

HEY !
YAHIKO-KUN.
HEY, HAVE YOU SEEN SANOSUKE ?
HE WAS JUST HERE, TRASHING THE PLACE.

...SAY.
HOW'S KAORU-CHAN DOING?

NOT GOOD.
IT'S LIKE SHE JUST LOST HER SPIRIT.
I GUESS HE JUST FLAT-OUT SAID FAREWELL.

THANK YOU FOR EVERYTHING AND...
SAYONARA.

THIS ONE IS RUROUNI.
ONCE AGAIN...
...THIS ONE WILL DRIFT.

SOBB...

GAAAAH!!

I UNDERSTAND HOW YOU FEEL, BUT WILL YOU PLEASE JUST DIG YOURSELF OUT?!

THIS ISN'T LIKE YOU! EITHER GO AFTER HIM OR FORGET HIM!

SNIF
HEY... C'MON...
...

SHE HASN'T EATEN A THING FOR TWO DAYS NOW.
OH...

MAYBE IF YOU TWO DROPPED IN TO CHEER HER UP...
OF COURSE.

READ THIS WAY

...
TM TM TM

月岡
TSUKIOKA
THIS SHOULD BE PLENTY TO GET TO KYOTO.
SHP

THANKS. I'LL PAY YOU BACK WHEN I RETURN...
DUNNO HOW...
YOU'RE WELCOME, AND IT'S MY PLEASURE.
I WON'T HOLD MY BREATH.

GIVE ME YOUR HAND.
?

READ THIS WAY

A FAREWELL GIFT. TAKE IT.
BOMP
BOMP
BOMBS.
YOU'VE BEEN MAKING *THIS* STUFF AGAIN-?!
OOH, NEW DESIGN.
DON'T WORRY. THEY'RE JUST FOR PROTECTION.

BE CAREFUL, SANOSUKE.

THE KYOTO OF TODAY IS A MORE *DANGEROUS PLACE* THAN YOU THINK.

YOU ALREADY KNOW ABOUT SHISHIO...?

NEVER UNDER-ESTIMATE WHAT A JOURNALIST HEARS.

JUST DON'T *WRITE* ABOUT IT.

IT'LL GET YOU MORE THAN JUST TROUBLE WITH THE LAW.

I WON'T. NO ONE WOULD BELIEVE IT ANY-WAY.

KLATTA

YEAH. YOU'RE PROBABLY RIGHT.

MWUG
PBT
AND WHERE ARE YOU RUNNING TO?
YOU SHOULD TALK! WHAT ARE YOU WANDERING AROUND FOR?!
I'VE NEEDED YOU!
KAORU IS A MESS!!
I CAN'T HELP HER!
YAHIKO, YOU...
...YOU'VE BEEN FOLLOWED.

WHERE DO YOU PLAN ON GOING?
TO KYOTO, OF COURSE.
GOT A PROBLEM?

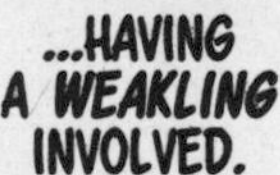

TO BATTŌSAI, YOUR EXISTENCE...

...IS NOTHING BUT A VULNERABILITY.

...

I TOOK ON THE ROLE OF JIN-E AND ATTACKED YOU IN ORDER TO DRIVE THAT POINT HOME.
GO TO KYOTO, AND IT WAS FOR NOTHING.
DON'T RUIN THIS BY FOLLOWING.
STAY PUT IN TOKYO.
...
I SEE. TO KENSHIN, I'M A LIABILITY...
...AND THAT'S WHY HE LEFT ON HIS OWN.

GOOD TO KNOW!

NOW I'M *REALLY* GONNA BELT HIM!!

MOVE, SAITŌ!

IF YOU DON'T MOVE, I'LL *MAKE* YOU!!

NO. YOU WILL NOT.

TP TP TP

YAAR!

URAAH!!

READ THIS WAY
!
TK
HMPH.

GUH
...
BLOOSH!
NO FAIR! HIS WOUND HADN'T HEALED YET!
VSH
!
BAM
WHAM!

READ THIS WAY
UNH...
G-G-G-
!!

I TOLD YOU.
THE ESSENCE OF COMBAT IS TO STRIKE THE VULNERA-BILITIES OF ONE'S OPPONENT.

THERE IS NO "FAIR" OR "UNFAIR."
BLUCH
KENSHIN DOESN'T GO TO A DOJO DUEL IN KYOTO. HE GOES TO A *DEATH MATCH.*

THIS IS NOT FOR YOU.
STAY HERE IN TOKYO.

READ THIS WAY
NEVER!
HNN
...
...AH.
NO PAIN HERE.
WOBBLE
PAIN TAKES TIME.
THIS WOUND...
...MIGHT HURT...
!

...BUT THAT PAIN'S *NOTHING* COMPARED TO KNOWING...
...THAT KENSHIN THINKS OF ME AS *WEAK!!*
ZAM
GHHH ...

SO, OUTTA MY WAY, SAITŌ!
I'M GOING TO KYOTO!
I'LL SHOW KENSHIN WHAT A "WEAKNESS" I AM...
...I'LL SHOW HIM WITH MY FISTS!
HUH...
TSK
THEN YOU SEAL HIS FATE.

Rurouni
Kenshin

Act 59
To
Kyoto
(Part II)

"SHOW HIM WITH YOUR FISTS"...
...DID YOU SAY?
YOU HEARD ME!!
YOU LIVE IN DREAMS.
REMEMBER HOW EASILY I BEAT YOU?
WHAT?!
NNG!
IT'S A TAUNT! BRUSH IT OFF!
CHK

FSSH

I WON'T LET YOU USE THE CHOICE OF WEAPONS AS AN EXCUSE THIS TIME.
THIS TIME, WE'LL FIGHT YOUR WAY...

...WITH FISTS.

READ THIS WAY

DON'T TRUST HIM, SANOSUKE!
HE'S SO DIRTY, HE'LL PROBABLY START KICKING YOU!
JAB
HUH...YOU REALLY DON'T LIKE ME, DO YOU.
WELL, DUH!
RRG!

YOU HAVE MY WORD. FISTS ONLY.
FAP
NO MATTER HOW STUPID THIS CHICKEN-HEAD MAY BE, IF HE'S CRUSHED AT HIS OWN STYLE OF COMBAT...
...EVENTUALLY HE'LL ACCEPT...
...HIS OWN WORTH...
...OR LACK OF IT.
THEN TRY IT!

HERE!
RRAH !!
A FULL SWING AFTER LUNGING.
A FOOL'S ONLY TRICK.

WE'LL JUST SEE...
...WHO'S THE FOOL, HERE!!
MULTI-BLOWS!
SINCE WHEN DID HE LEARN THAT?!

WITH A SWORD, YOU CAN PARRY AND GO STRAIGHT TO THE ATTACK...
...BUT YOU CAN'T DO ANYTHING WHEN YOU BLOCK A FIST!
IF I ATTACK CONSTANTLY, YOU CAN'T COUNTER—
...AND IF YOU CAN'T COUNTER, EVENTUALLY I BEAT YOU DOWN!!
THOUGH I'VE GOTTA ADMIT, JUST THROWING OUT THE ODD PUNCH...
...IS KINDA EMBARRASSING.

HUH.
!
AND IF YOU NEVER LAND A BLOW?
SMIRK
...NOT EVEN ONE HIT?!
YOU ARE AMUSING.

READ THIS WAY
SANOSUKE!
DDDDDDDDDDDDM
!!
UNGH...THE SPEED OF OUR PUNCHES IS HARDLY DIFFERENT...
SO HOW COME MINE DON'T HIT AND HIS DO ...?!
WHY ...??

DMSCH
HE'S GOOD.
SORRY TO SAY, BUT YEAH.
HE'S THE ONLY ONE I'VE EVER SEEN IN KENSHIN'S LEAGUE.
YOU GET IT NOW?
YOU CANNOT APPROACH ME...
...OR BATTŌSAI IN ABILITY AND EXPERIENCE.
YOU ARE A HATCHLING.
LIVELY AND LAUGHABLE.

SHUT UP!
I DON'T CARE!

I'M GOING TO KYOTO—
HHHH

...NO MATTER WHO TELLS ME NOT TO.
HPP

WOBBLE!!
!

THAT BLOW TO YOUR CHIN SEEMS TO HAVE AFFECTED YOUR BRAIN.

HUPP

YOU WILL *NOT* GO TO KYOTO.

HEY!

HE'S NOT HOLDING A SWORD— BUT THAT'S STILL THE *GATOTSU* STANCE!

DODGE IT, SANOSUKE!

THAT'LL TAKE YOU DOWN!!

HE CAN'T. HE'S BARELY STANDING AS IT IS.

NO MATTER HOW HARD YOU FIGHT...

YOU'RE STILL A HATCHLING.
NOTHING MORE!!

YOUR POINT BEING ??!
HUK
KKKK
EH...?

READ THIS WAY
HOW'S THAT? LOOKS LIKE EVEN A HATCHLING...
...CAN STILL BREAK AN ARM, HUH?
HEH
YOU...

YOU KEEP CALLING ME "HATCHLING"
KK
KK
KK
SO WHAT ARE YOU?

I DON'T CARE HOW MUCH EXPERIENCE YOU HAVE, NEITHER YOU NOR KENSHIN WAS THIS STRONG TO START WITH.
TEN YEARS AGO, YOU WERE JUST A KILLER YOURSELF.
NOW YOU'RE POWERFUL ENOUGH TO INFLUENCE THE DIRECTION OF THE GOVERNMENT.

EVEN A "HATCHLING"...
...CAN GET IN A PECK OR TWO.

YOU...

TP

...ENOUGH.

NN?!

!

HMF.

YOU WIN, SANOSUKE.

TP
TP

...

HEY. LET'S TREAT THOSE WOUNDS. THAT SHOULDER LOOKS BAD.
UH HUH...

SS

?
SOMETHING WRONG, SANOSUKE?
悪

THAT PUNK. WITH ALL THE PUNCHES HE THREW...
...HE DIDN'T THROW ONE AT MY SHOULDER.
HE LITERALLY WAS...
...FIGHTING AT MY LEVEL.
A SHINSEN-GUMI CAPTAIN...
A "WOLF OF MIBU," THEY CALLED HIM. I SEE WHY.
DAMN IT!
I CAN'T BE WASTING TIME AROUND HERE! I'M GOING!!
BUT WHAT ABOUT YOUR...?
I'LL SEE TO 'EM ON THE WAY.
JUST GIMME THE MEDICINE!

THE REST IS UP TO YOU, YAHIKO.
I DO THINK YOU'D BETTER...
...GET THE LITTLE MISS TO KENSHIN SOMEHOW.
...AGREED!
I'VE GOT TO BE STRONGER!!
WHY DON'T MINE HIT AND HIS DO...?!
A FOOL WHO RELIES SO MUCH ON HIS OWN TOUGHNESS THAT HE LEARNS NOTHING OF DEFENSE HAS NOTHING TO RELY ON.
I'VE GOTTA FIGURE IT OUT...
...BEFORE I GET TO KYOTO!!

Rurouni
Kenshin

## Act 60
# Megumi's Feelings•Kaoru's Feelings

I COULDN'T CHASE AFTER HIM.

I DON'T KNOW WHY...

...BUT THAT ONE WORD FROM HIM... "SAYONARA"...

...THAT PARALYZED ME.

AND THAT'S STILL...

...ALL I CAN HEAR.

# Act 60

## Megumi's Feelings •Kaoru's Feelings

READ THIS WAY
剣術道場
I KNOW HOW YOU FEEL, KAORU-CHAN...
...BUT YOU CAN'T JUST WALLOW LIKE THIS.
IT'S TIME TO WAKE UP.
RUMMAGE RUMMAGE
...I KNOW!
I'LL GIVE YOU THESE: "IBAHACHI" BY TSUNAN, AND...
GRIN
..."HIJIKATA TOSHIZO" BY NAKAJIMA NOBORI. THEY'RE MY TREASURES!
土方歳三
KSSSH
WHO WANTS THAT GARBAGE?

"GARBAGE" ...
MY TREASURES ARE GARBAGE.
GLOO OOM
...

YAHIKO?!
I'M SHOCKED, I THOUGHT YOU'D BE GOING TO KYOTO.
LOOKING AFTER THE DOJO ALONE?
HUH?
WHAT ARE YOU TALKING ABOUT? KAORU'S STILL THERE.

...I'M AFRAID THIS ISN'T VERY GOOD, BUT

...IT'S BAD FOR YOU NOT TO EAT ANYTHING.

DON'T WANT IT.

WILL YOU STOP THIS?

TSUBAME-CHAN MADE IT FOR YOU.

KLAK

I SAID, I DON'T WANT IT.

KAORU-CHAN!!

JUST STOP BOTHER-ING ME!!

PLEASE JUST LEAVE ME ALONE!!

READ THIS WAY
MEGUMI-SAN!

I'M DISAPPOINTED.
YOU'RE STILL HERE.

NPFH...
WHAT ABOUT *YOU*?

WHAT ELSE?
HO HO HO
I CAME TO *LAUGH* AT THE *LOSER* WHO GOT DUMPED BY KENSHIN!
...
WITCH...
T-TAKANI-SAN...!!

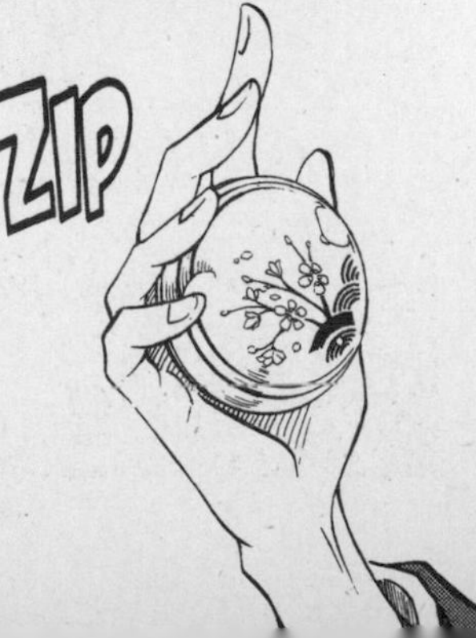
ZIP

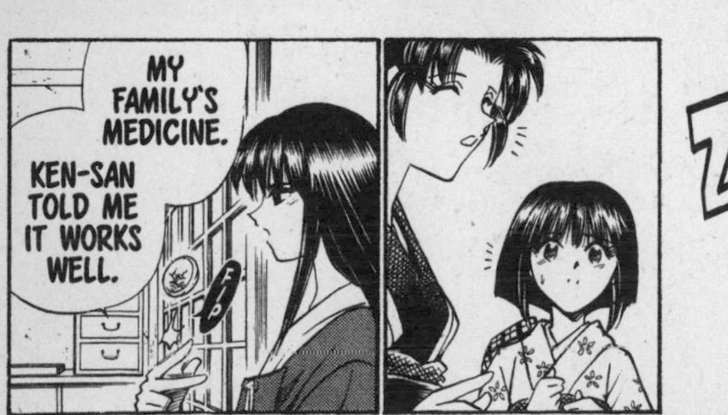
MY FAMILY'S MEDICINE.
KEN-SAN TOLD ME IT WORKS WELL.

READ
THIS
WAY

I THINK HE MAY NEED IT, BUT ASKING YOU TO GET IT TO HIM WOULD BE A WASTE...
...SO, I'LL GIVE IT TO YAHIKO-KUN.
PIF
WHY DON'T YOU STOP DEPENDING ON OTHERS AND TAKE IT TO KYOTO...
...BY YOURSELF?
HSS

WOMEN AT WAR...
...
...
SCARY! SCA-A-ARY--!

UN-FORTUNATELY, I'M A DOCTOR.
I HAVE RESPONSI-BILITIES... UNLIKE YOU.
AH. SO YOUR PATIENTS ARE MORE IMPORTANT THAN KENSHIN...!
I GUESS THAT SHOWS HOW YOU FEEL ABOUT HIM.
KAORU-CHAN...
REALLY, NOW, MUST YOU—?

WHAK
I'M THE MASTER OF A DOJO!
DON'T YOU MAKE LIGHT OF—
VNN
!

YOU'RE THE ONE MAKING LIGHT...
GNG

MY OBLIGATION'S NOT ONLY TO MY *PATIENTS*, BUT ALSO TO THOSE I *HARMED* IN MY FORMER LIFE.
IT'S THE PATH I WALK—
—AND THE ONE WHO SHOWED IT TO ME WAS *KENSHIN*.
I...
PWIK

WHATEVER MAY HAPPEN, WHETHER KEN-SAN STAYS OR GOES, I *WILL* FOLLOW THE PATH OF A DOCTOR.
*THAT* IS HOW I SHOW MY FEELINGS FOR KEN-SAN.

IF YOU WANT TO HONOR HIS MEMORY BY SITTING ON YOUR BUTT AND SULKING, THEN PLEASE DO.
PWIP

...

*SNORT* AND YOUR ONLY REACTION IS TO CRY?

YOU ARE A WEAKLING.

...YOU CAN'T UNDERSTAND.

YOU COULD NEVER UNDERSTAND HOW IT FELT...

...HAVING HIM SAY GOODBYE TO MY FACE!!

...

YOU'RE RIGHT.

YOU DONE TALKING TO HER?

WE'LL BRING KENSHIN BACK... SOMEHOW.
DON'T WORRY.
YES.

DON'T CRY, OKAY? JUST YOU WAIT.

SURE...
CAN YOU UNDERSTAND KNOWING HE *LEFT* WITHOUT EVEN *BOTHERING* TO SAY IT?

READ THIS WAY

HEY, WHAT'S TAKING YOU SO LONG?!

SLAM

I THOUGHT YOU'D BE *READY*!

!

AREN'T WE GOING—

—TO KYOTO ?!

BUT...

NO "*BUT*"! YOU'RE THE ONLY ONE KENSHIN SAID GOODBYE TO, RIGHT?

DON'T YOU GET IT? THAT MEANS, FOR KENSHIN...
...PARTING WITH YOU WAS THE HARDEST!
NO MATTER WHO SAYS WHAT, YOU'RE OUR BEST HOPE FOR BRINGING HIM BACK!
MEGUMI'LL TAKE CARE OF THE DOJO WHILE WE'RE GONE...
GRP
...AND, IN EXCHANGE, YOU'RE GONNA HAND THIS TO KENSHIN!
ANSWER ME, KAORU!
DO YOU WANT TO SEE HIM OR NOT?!
I...
I...!
KAORU-CHAN!
KAORU-SAN!!

...I WANT TO SEE HIM.
DRIP
I REALLY...
DROP
...REALLY WANT TO SEE HIM!

TO KYOTO— TO KENSHIN!

READ THIS WAY

SO...

...I GET LEFT BEHIND.

AND ON TOP OF EVERYTHING ELSE, I HAVE TO TAKE CARE OF THE DAMN DOJO.

THAT'S WHAT I GET FOR BEING SO...

KREEE

!

KATA

IT'S OPEN... BUT HOW? I HAVE THE KEYS!

DID YAHIKO COME BACK FOR SOME-THING HE FORGOT...?

OR...

...COULD IT BE...

TM TM TM TM TM

AND JUST WHERE...

...DID BATTŌSAI GO?

Rurouni Kenshin

READ THIS WAY

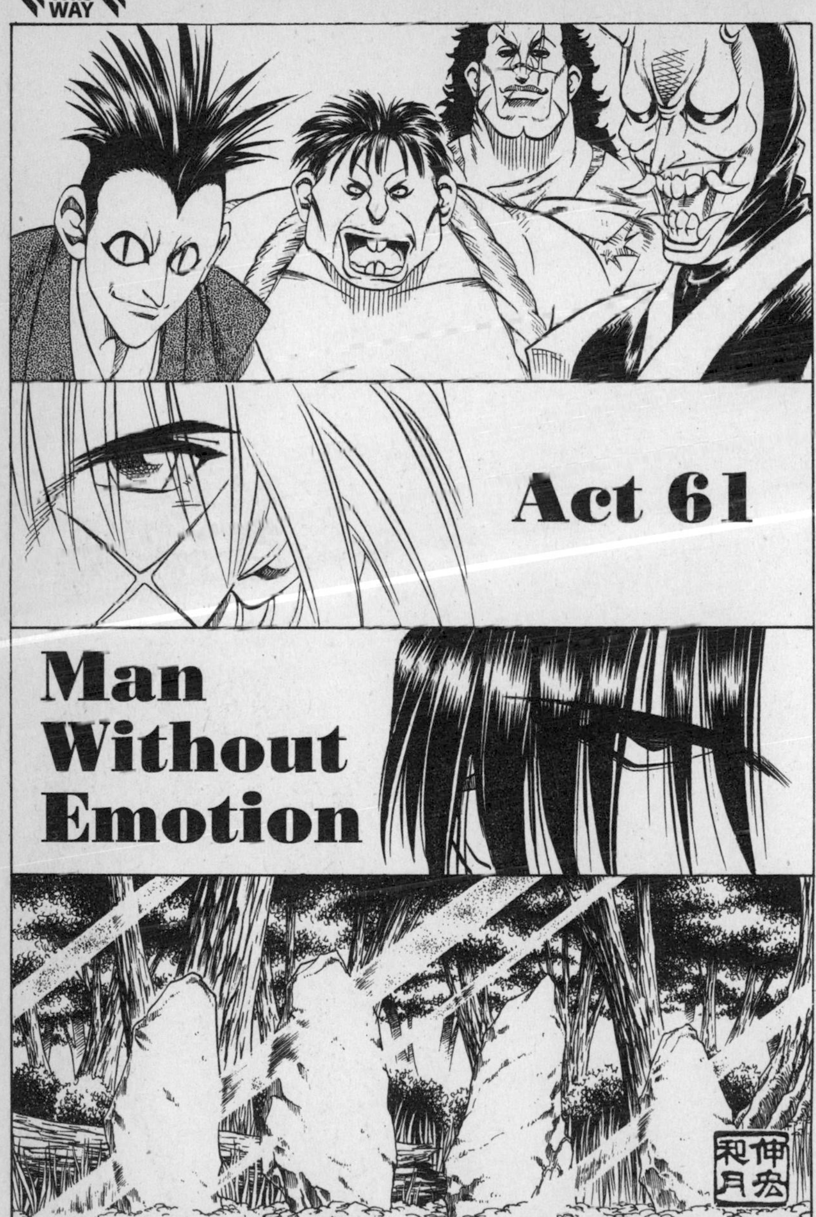
Act 61
Man Without Emotion

WHERE. IS. BATTŌSAI?
TP
UH...
AH...
HYOOOOH
GAAN
GEEA

READ THIS WAY

IF YOU DON'T ANSWER...

I WILL KILL YOU.

...

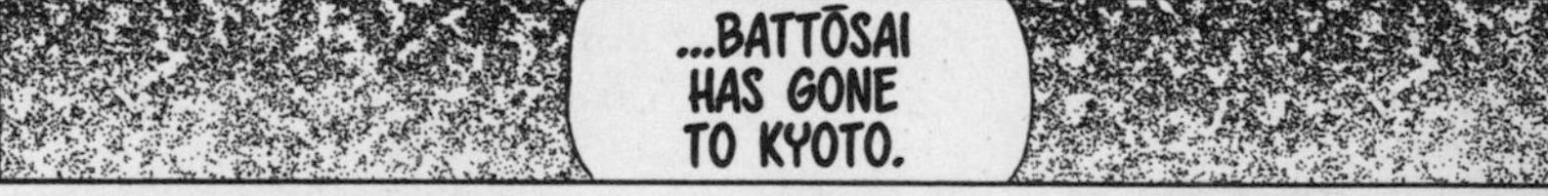

READ THIS WAY

...AND YOU ARE?

FUJITA GORŌ.

JUST A POLICE-MAN, AS YOU CAN SEE.

...

DON'T LOOK SO ANGRY.

I'M ABOUT TO TELL YOU WHAT'S BEEN HAPPENING WHILE YOU WERE IN THE MOUNTAINS.

...ALL RIGHT.

START TALKING.

—...

READ THIS WAY

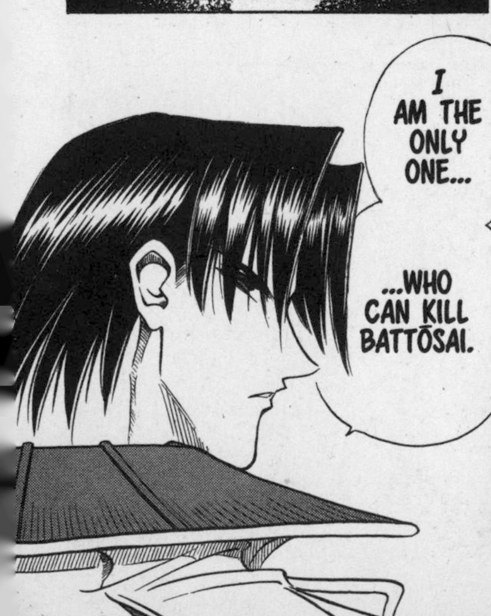

READ THIS WAY

SUCH CON-FIDENCE.
STILL...
I WOULD NOT CALL IT OVER-CONFIDENCE.

WHAT DID YOU TELL HIM ALL THAT FOR?!
RRR!
YOU'RE GOING TO GET KEN-SAN KILLED!

NOW, NOW. IF I HADN'T TOLD HIM, HE'D HAVE KILLED YOU.
MMG!

A MAN DOESN'T BECOME HEAD OF THE ONIWABANSHŪ AT THE AGE OF 15 WITHOUT TRUE GREATNESS.
I CAN USE A MAN THAT SKILLED.

...
...
YOUR THOUGHTS ...
I AGREE.

THIS SHINOMORI AOSHI...

TP

...HE CERTAINLY DOES SEEM USEFUL.

GULP

GULP

...YEAH, SHE WAS A GOOD ONE.

HEH!

I WANNA GET WITH HER NEXT TIME.

HEY.
HERE HE COMES.

YOU'RE LATE. WE'RE TIRED OF WAITING.
YOU MUST BE SHINOMORI AOSHI.
...AND YOU?

WE ARE THE CHOSEN OF THE GREAT SHISHIO.

THE FOUR PRIESTS OF ABUKUMA.

...

BE HONORED. THE MASTER HAS ASKED TO MEET WITH YOU PERSONALLY.

EVEN WE MAY ONLY MEET WITH HIM ONCE A YEAR... IF THAT.

THIS MUST NOT BE TAKEN LIGHTLY.

HURRY, THEN.
YOU KEEP MASTER SHISHIO WAITING.

READ THIS WAY

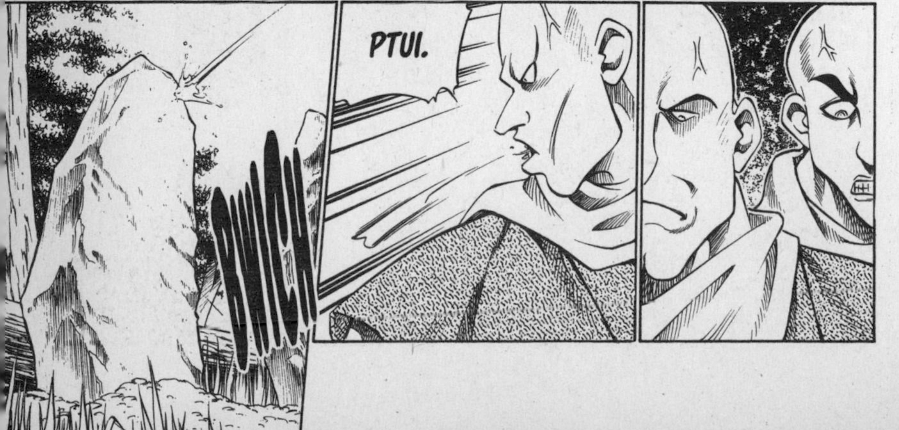

BE CAREFUL, FOOL.
TO SAY YOU WILL KILL *US* IS INSULT ENOUGH. BUT THE MAN...
...WHO SAYS HE WOULD KILL *MASTER SHISHIO*...
...DE-SERVES TO DIE...
...A THOUSAND DEATHS!
NO MAN CAN INSULT THE MASTER...
...MORE THAN ONCE!!
HSH

A LONG SWORD ...!!
HAS HE CHANGED WEAPONS SINCE HE LOST TO BATTOSAI?!
WHATEVER HE WIELDS...
...HE WON'T BE ABLE TO BLOCK FOUR ATTACKS ALL TOGETHER!
!
TWO SHORT SWORDS IN ONE SHEATH !!
COULD THIS BE—?!

"KODACHI NITŌ-RYŪ." THE DUAL KATANA.
GLORIOUS.
YOU DIDN'T EVEN GIVE THEM TIME TO MAKE THEIR SYNCHRONOUS ATTACK.
TP
ARE YOU ANOTHER OF SHISHIO'S MEN?

YES.

SETA SŌJIRŌ.

FEW ARE AS CLOSE TO THE MASTER AS I.

YOU IMPRESS ME.

I HOPE YOU ARE WILLING AT LEAST TO COME AND—

SAVE YOUR BREATH.

I HAVE NO NEED OF ALLIES.

ESPECIALLY A MAN COLD ENOUGH TO THROW HIS MEN AWAY TO TEST ANOTHER'S STRENGTH.
AH. SO YOU KNOW ABOUT THAT.
YES. THE MASTER PUT THEM AT RISK...
STILL...
HOW *COLD* IS THE MAN WHO SLICED THEM TO PIECES WITHOUT HESITATION...
...EVEN THOUGH HE *KNEW* THEIR PURPOSE?

...

HSSH

...WELL. YOU WILL BE WELCOME IN KYOTO, SHOULD YOU CHOOSE TO COME.
WHRR
WE SHALL BE WAITING THERE.
TK
TO MISS TWO *TURNING POINTS* IN HISTORY, WITHIN THE SPACE OF A FEW YEARS...
SURELY, TO THE OKASHIRA OF THE ONIWABANSHŪ, *THAT* WOULD BE A *DISGRACE.*

...
TK
TK
AND HOW...
...IS THIS ONE?
TK

I LIKE HIM.

I LIKE A WARRIOR WHO CAN CHOP MEN LIKE FIREWOOD.

READ THIS WAY

WELL ENOUGH.

Rurouni
Kenshin

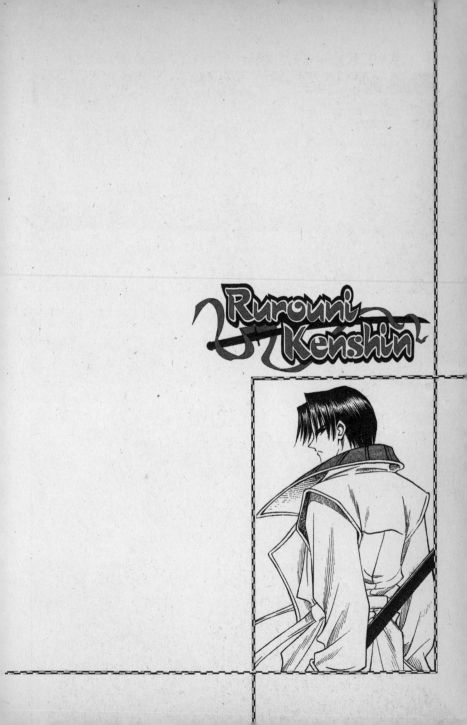

# Act 62—On the East Sea Road

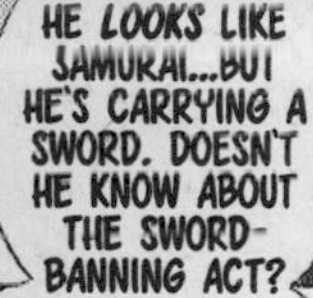


WE'D BEST KEEP OUR DISTANCE, JUST IN CASE...

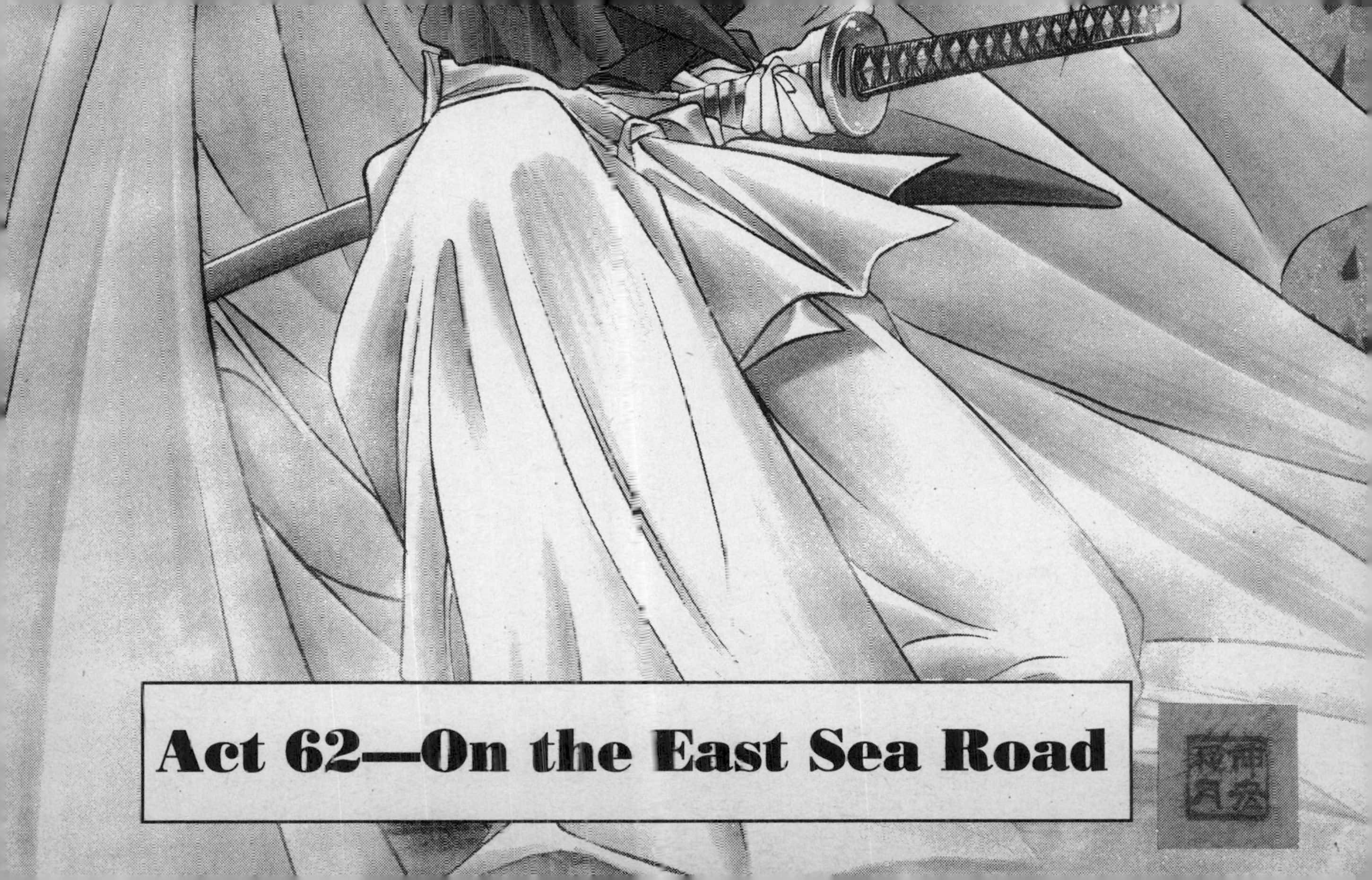
Act 62—On the East Sea Road

OH...
ZP
A KATANA!
HSST! HUSH, NOW.
SHH!
TP
TP
IT'S A KATANA!
HE'S DANGEROUS.
STAY AWAY FROM HIM!

DID YOU SAY YOUR FAREWELLS TO THE KAMIYA GIRL?

ANYHOW, COME WITH ME.
TP
IF WE LEAVE FOR YOKOHAMA NOW, WE'LL BE ABLE TO MAKE THE MORNING BOAT TO OSAKA.

NO.
THIS ONE WILL BE TAKING THE EAST SEA ROAD.

WHAT, YOU DON'T HAVE THE FARE? THE GOVERNMENT WILL PAY—
THAT'S *NOT* IT.

YOU SAW WITH ŌKUBO'S MURDER THAT SHISHIO'S MEN ARE ABLE TO *APPEAR* AND *DISAPPEAR* AS THEY PLEASE.
THEY MAY WELL *AMBUSH* US ON THE BOAT.

IF WE HAVE TO FIGHT THEM THERE...
...WE'LL PUT INNOCENT PEOPLE AT RISK.
YOU'RE STILL THINKING LIKE "RUROUNI."
IT WOULD BE BETTER IF YOU'D STOP BEING SO *STUPID* AND BECOME "*HITOKIRI*" ONCE MORE.
SHALL WE GO AT IT AGAIN?

HSH
IF IT'S A FIGHT YOU SEEK, YOU MAY HAVE IT...
...BUT THIS ONE HAS NO INTENTION OF BECOMING *BATTŌSAI* EVER AGAIN.
NO ONE ELSE CAN BE INVOLVED IN THIS BATTLE.
*THAT* IS WHY THIS ONE ACTS ALONE.
...
JUST DON'T DAWDLE, ALL RIGHT?
...ALL RIGHT. IT DOESN'T MATTER WHICH ROAD YOU TAKE, SO LONG AS YOU GET TO KYOTO.
IT WOULD TAKE THE *AVERAGE PERSON* AT LEAST TEN DAYS...
...BUT FOR YOU, FIVE SHOULD BE *PLENTY.*
SHISHIO HAS SPUN A *SPIDER'S WEB* OF INTELLIGENCE ACROSS THE NATION.
HE'LL KNOW *ALL* THAT YOU DO.
ZZ

"DO NOT FORGET, THE BATTLE AGAINST SHISHIO...

"...HAS ALREADY BEGUN."

"TO WALK WITH THE SWORD WORN OPENLY, THERE WILL BE *AVOIDANCE*, OUT OF *FEAR*.

"NO ONE WILL GET MIXED UP IN—"

PWEE! PEE!

ORORO.

YOU!! YOUNG MAN!!

HEYY!

HOW *DARE* YOU VIOLATE THE SWORD BAN—AND *RIGHT* IN MY *FACE*!!

PWEE!

...

T-T

T-T-T-T-

T-T-

...

STRETCHING NEARLY 500KM FROM THE JAPAN BRIDGE (NIHONBASHI) TO THE SANJŌ Ō BRIDGE IN KYOTO— THE EAST SEA ROAD (TŌKAIDŌ) HAS BEEN AN IMPORTANT ROUTE SINCE ANCIENT TIMES.

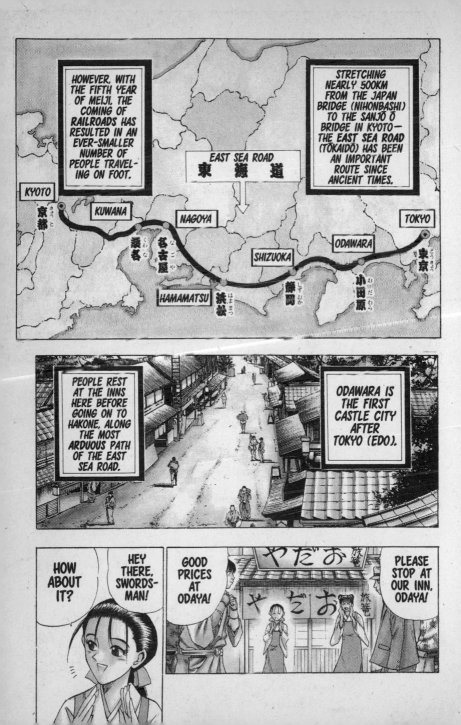

HOWEVER, WITH THE FIFTH YEAR OF MEIJI, THE COMING OF RAILROADS HAS RESULTED IN AN EVER-SMALLER NUMBER OF PEOPLE TRAVELING ON FOOT.

EAST SEA ROAD
東海道

TOKYO 東京 とうきょう
ODAWARA 小田原 おだわら
SHIZUOKA 静岡 しずおか
HAMAMATSU 浜松 はままつ
NAGOYA 名古屋 なごや
KUWANA 桑名 くわな
KYOTO 京都 きょうと

ODAWARA IS THE FIRST CASTLE CITY AFTER TOKYO (EDO).
PEOPLE REST AT THE INNS HERE BEFORE GOING ON TO HAKONE, ALONG THE MOST ARDUOUS PATH OF THE EAST SEA ROAD.

PLEASE STOP AT OUR INN, ODAYA!
旅篭 おだや
GOOD PRICES AT ODAYA!
HEY THERE, SWORDSMAN!
HOW ABOUT IT?

SORRY, IN A HURRY.

A HURRY? BUT IT'S ALMOST SUNSET.
NIGHT WILL COME ON YOU IN THE MOUNTAINS!

STOPPING AT AN INN COULD INVOLVE THEM IN TROUBLE.
MEN WITH SWORDS AREN'T SO UNCOMMON THIS FAR FROM TOKYO, IT SEEMS.

CONTACT WITH PEOPLE MUST BE AVOIDED, AS MUCH AS POSSIBLE...

HE MUST BE FLAT BROKE.
PFT.
...

READ THIS WAY

WELL, NOW.

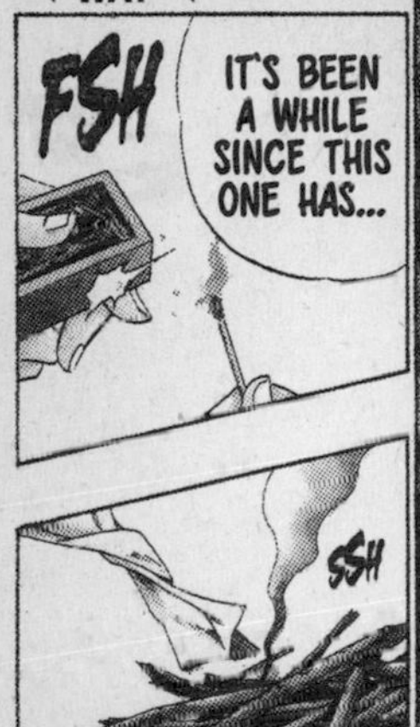
FSH
IT'S BEEN A WHILE SINCE THIS ONE HAS...
SSH

...
KRACKLE KRACKLE

THEY MUST ALL BE...
...FURIOUS BY NOW.

...

WORSE...
...THEY'VE EVERY *REASON* TO BE.

A GIRL'S VOICE...AND SEVERAL MEN.

THEY COULDN'T BE SHISHIO'S MEN...

...

...

BANDITS... OR THIEVES.
TP...
PEOPLE MUST BE AVOIDED...
...BUT THIS CAN'T BE IGNORED.

FMP
YAAH!
HEH HEH.
HEY, GIRL.
WHY SO FRIGHTENED, EH?

YOU'RE THE ONE WHO INVITED US.
HEH
...ALL RIGHT, THEN.
BUT ARE YOU SURE YOU HAVE MONEY?



WE JUST FINISHED SOME "BUSINESS" IN ODAWARA.
OF COURSE WE DO.
JANGLE
GOOD FOR YOU.
GRAB
UH?
AND NOW...
FWAH

THE SHOW IS OVER!

GIVE ME ALL YOUR MONEY!

RR
...EH ...?
RR
SUCH A SEXY VOICE, TOO...SURE RAISED MY HOPES.
GO HOME, WASH YOUR FACE, AND GO TO BED, KID.
RRROWRR!
HOLD IT!!
WHAT PART OF THIS IS A "KID"?!
HUH, YOU BLIND MEN?!
YOU... YOU BRAT!

I'LL HAVE YOU KNOW ...
...I'M 16!!
GWAH!
THHG
WATCH YOURSELF, KID!!
VSSH
!
WE'RE ALREADY WANTED FOR ROBBERY!
YOU THINK A MURDER OR TWO COUNTS NOW??
TAKE THIS!
VSH
DM

READ THIS WAY
!!!
NO MAN WHO DEPENDS ON STRENGTH ALONE...
...WILL EVER BE ABLE TO CAPTURE ME.
U... WAH !!

READ THIS WAY

WELL. WHAT A SURPRISE.

!!!

PWIYK

A ROBBERY WAS ONE THING...

...BUT WHO'D HAVE THOUGHT A *DAMSEL IN DISTRESS*...

...WOULD BE DOING THE *ROBBING*?

OH, SO...
...GIRLS AREN'T SUPPOSED TO STEAL, IS THAT IT?
NOT AT ALL.
B-BMP
B-BMP
NOT JUST GIRLS.
NO ONE SHOULD BE STEALING.
OHO. SO YOU THINK YOU CAN TELL ME WHAT TO DO...?
THEN MAYBE I'LL STEAL YOUR MONEY, TOO.
OF COURSE, LOOKING AT YOU...
...I DON'T THINK YOU HAVE ANY.
...
DOES IT EVER END?
WELL, THEN, IF YOU ARE BROKE...
...I GUESS I'LL JUST HAVE TO TAKE...
...THAT SWORD OF YOURS, INSTEAD!
ORORO?

Rurouni Kenshin

Act 63
Makimachi Misao
伸宏和月

SWORD...?
YUP.
IF YOU RISK CARRYING IT AGAINST THE LAW, IT MUST BE WORTH *SOMETHING*...
SP
...RIGHT?
WHOA!

!
YAHH!!!
HOW'S THAT?!
HOW'S... WHAT?
THO' IT DID HURT A LITTLE.
BLOWS FROM AN AMATEUR LIKE YOU WOULDN'T HAVE ANY FORCE BEHIND THEM EVEN IF YOU DID HIT.
JANGLE
AAAH?!
LET'S STOP NOW. THIS MONEY SHOULD—

READ THIS WAY
NOW I'M MAD!
RRR
RRR
GIVE IT BACK!
THAT'S MINE!!
!
FSST
TAKE THIS!
KANSATSU TOBIKUNAI!
YAH!

THP
THP
THP
THP
THP
THP
AUGH! MY CLOAK!!
OH...
SORRY...
GLOOB
GIMME BACK MY MONEY AND MY CLOAK!!
THE CLOAK, SURE. BUT THE MONEY ISN'T REALLY YOURS, IS IT?
RRROWR!
I STOLE IT, SO IT'S MINE!!
...
THE LEAST YOU CAN DO IS PAY ME FOR MY CLOAK!
GIMME YOUR SWORD! THEN WE'RE EVEN!!

READ THIS WAY

HMM
MM

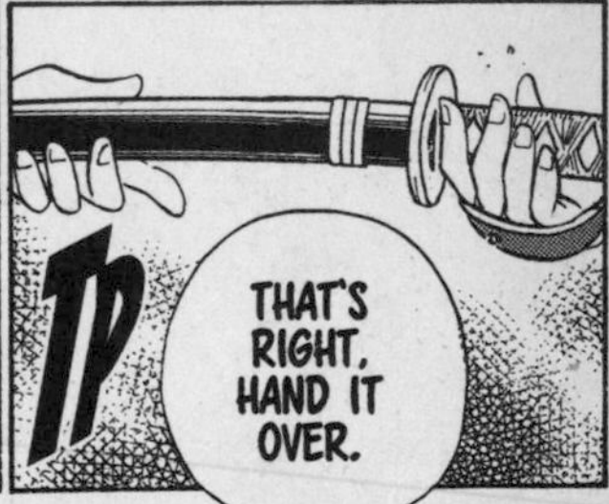
TP
THAT'S RIGHT, HAND IT OVER.

ALL RIGHT, LET'S HAVE A LOOK...

VNN
HUH?
THE BLADE'S UPSIDE-DOWN...

AS YOU CAN SEE...
...THAT'S NOT A NORMAL SWORD.
IF YOU TRY TO SELL IT, YOU'LL HARDLY GET SMALL CHANGE.

HMM...
WELL... I CAN ALWAYS USE SMALL CHANGE.
ORO ?!?!
CHEEN
I'LL TAKE IT.

Long time no see! Watsuki here. I don't have the usual ball-point pen handy, so for today, it's fine-point. ...So, "Rurouni Kenshin" is about to be adapted to animation! I know a lot of people will object... and I understand the objections. I've had two or three favorite manga ruined by horrible artwork and storylines in the course of being animated, myself. But, for a manga artist like Watsuki—for whom the artwork is kind of "anime-esque" already—this is a dream. It all happened really fast, and the production schedule is tight, so I've got my worries...but please try and keep an open heart, and an open mind, all right?

伸宏和月

KLINK

小田原宿
田村屋

ODAWARA INN

"ODAWARA INN."

"TAMURA CURRENCY EXCHANGE."

両替

小田原宿
田村屋

THIS MUST BE IT.

IT LOOKS LIKE THEY HAVEN'T EVEN NOTICED THE ROBBERY.

SO MUCH THE BETTER FOR US.

HMPH.

READ THIS WAY
BAM
HO. NOT BAD, NOT BAD 'TALL.
...
I GET IT. YOU'RE A BANDIT TOO, HUH?
WELL, YOU'RE NOT THE ONLY ONE WHO—
NG...
YAH!!
!
TOOM!
HOW'S ZAT?
HEH

READ THIS WAY

HER MARTIAL-ARTS MOVES, THE THROWING DAGGERS...
THIS ISN'T THE NINJA-GIRL NEXT DOOR.
HER CLOTHES ARE WEIRD ENOUGH...
A BIT YOUNG, TO SHOW SO MUCH THIGH...?
HUH?

KCH
NOW, THEN...
...ALL IS WELL.
TING

IT SURE IS!
FUMP

—SO YOU'RE FROM KYOTO, THEN?

*UH-HUH!* AND, HALFWAY BACK FROM TOKYO, I RAN OUT OF MONEY, SO I *HAD* TO STEAL!

THEN *YOU* CAME, AND RUINED THINGS.

BUT WHAT WAS A YOUNG GIRL DOING...

...ALL ALONE IN TOKYO?

WELL...

I WAS *LOOKING* FOR SOMEONE.

A PERSON WHO, DURING THE BAKUMATSU...

...TOOK ME IN WHEN I HAD NO ONE ELSE AND RAISED ME.

AT THE START OF MEIJI, WE TRAVELED ALL OVER, BUT THEN...

...HE LEFT ME IN KYOTO WITH A FRIEND OF HIS, AN OLD MAN.

I WANTED TO *STAY* WITH HIM! EVERY TIME I HEAR THE RUMORS...

...I RUN AWAY FROM HOME TO *FIND* HIM!

BUT EACH TIME, I FAIL!

MISPLACED ANGER

GUH

GYOOO

AT LAST, THINGS BECOME CLEAR, *UH...*

...UH ...

...WHAT, MY NAME? MISAO.

MAKIMACHI MISAO.

STILL, NO MATTER HOW BADLY YOU NEED THE MONEY, YOU OUGHTN'T BE STEALING...
THEN HOW AM I S'PPOSED TO GET HOME, HUH?!
YOU HAVE THIS ONE'S MONEY, NOW.
USE IT TO SEND A LETTER TO THIS "OLD MAN" IN KYOTO, AND HAVE HIM COME FETCH YOU.
OHH, YEAH!
ANOTHER THING: THE MEN YOU ATTACKED PROBABLY HAVE YAKUZA CONNEC-TIONS...
...SO YOU'D BETTER GET OUT OF ODAWARA AS SOON AS...
THERE THEY ARE!!
!

GET OVER HERE!
TMTMTMTMTMTMTM
!
THEY'RE ALL OVER!
CUT THEM OFF!!
YOU WENCH...
...NOW YOU'LL PAY!
DM DM DM DM
FEH.
PUH-LEEZE.
THERE'S ABOUT 30.
THINK YOU CAN HANDLE HALF, SWORDSMAN?
GNG

OF ALL THE...!

THIS ONE WOULD PREFER TO STAY *OUT* OF THIS NONSENSE.

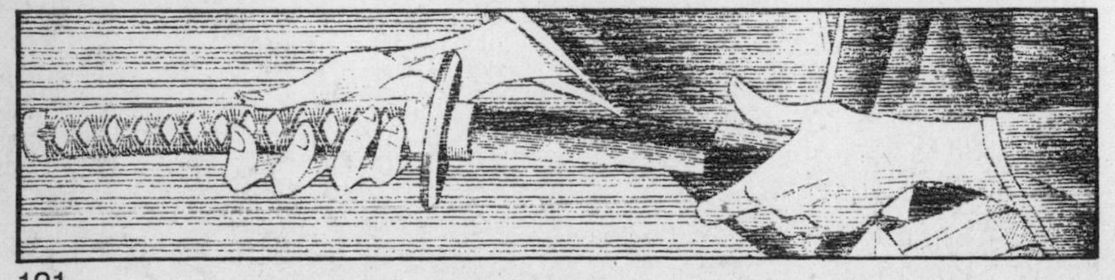

...!
YOU'RE ALL THIEVES... AND SHE'S A THIEF FOR STEALING FROM YOU.
SHP
WHAT SAY YOU THIS ONE CALLS IT EVEN, AND PUNISHES BOTH SIDES...?

KEEEN
GAAH !!!

HAH...

HOO...

HUH...

YOU MAY NOT *LOOK* LIKE MUCH...

...BUT, BOY HOWDY! YOU GOT IT WHERE IT *COUNTS.*

AND HOW!

KOF

THIS ONE'S DEFENDED HIS SHARE OF RIVERBANKS...

...AND DROPPING A BRIDGE IS EASY WHEN THE OPPONENTS PUT ALL THEIR *WEIGHT* IN THE *MIDDLE.*

THAT'S GREAT...

...*ALMOST* AS GREAT AS THE FOLKS WHO RAISED ME!

HEH
"ALMOST," HUH?
TP
YEAH. DURING THE BAKUMATSU...
...THEY DEFENDED THE *ROYAL EDO CASTLE* FROM THE SHADOWS.

Rurouni
Kenshin

...NO.
THAT IS A DIFFERENT MATTER.
QUIT JERKIN' ME AROUND ALREADY!
ORO ?!
ANSWER ME!
WHERE ARE AOSHI-SAMA AND—?!
MMMM
WOBBLE
WOBBLE
I WILL NOT GIVE UP!
HE'S THE FIRST SOLID LEAD TO AOSHI-SAMA AND THE OTHERS I'VE HAD...!
THO' I WILL REST...
箱根へ二里
HAKONE AHEAD

HEY!

HEY, WAIT UP!!
WHY ARE YOU SO SILENT ALL OF A SUDDEN?!

ANSWER ME! WHERE IS AOSHI-SAMA ?!
IS HAN'NYA-KUN OKAY ?!
WHAT ABOUT SHIKIJŌ-SAN? BESHIMI? HYOTTOKO?

TELL ME, YOU...
...CARROT-TOPPED...
NAG
...SCAR-FACED...
NAG
NAG
NAG
...GIRLY-MAN!!
NAG
...RED-DRESSED ...
...LAW-BREAKING ...
NAG
...

THERE IS A NAME: HIMURA KENSHIN.
PLEASE BE SO KIND AS TO USE IT.

IF I CALL YOU BY YOUR NAME...
PING
...WILL YOU TELL ME ABOUT THEM??

READ THIS WAY

SHINOMORI... AOSHI...

# Act 64—Playing "It"

YOU KNOW HIM...?
WHERE ARE THEY ALL NOW?! TELL ME!
ARE THEY ALIVE?!

SHE'S CERTAINLY PERSISTENT ...
TK
TK
TK
TK
SHOULD SHE BE TOLD OF THE ONIWABANSHŪ'S DEMISE...?

EVEN IF NOTHING IS SAID, EVENTUALLY SHE'LL KNOW.
IT WILL BREAK HER HEART... BUT IT MAY BE BETTER THAN HER SEARCHING FOREVER.

STILL...
UNTIL I COME KILL YOU, DON'T LET ANYONE BEAT ME TO IT."
...SHE'LL KEEP FOLLOWING, HOPING TO FIND ONE OF THEM.

HIKING WITH A HOPERUL *GIRL* IN TOW'S NO GOOD...
...NOT WHEN SHISHIO'S MEN COULD *ATTACK* AT ANY MOMENT.
SIGH...
SHE MUST BE LOST.
HUH?

READ THIS WAY

VM

DP

YAAAAH!

HEY!

KSH

KSH

READ
THIS
WAY

CHEEN
CHEEN
SLAPP
TSK.
SHE'S NOT GIVING UP...
GOT A GOOD PACE GOING, TOO. SHE MUST WANT TO SEE AOSHI BADLY.
IN THAT CASE...

FEH...

HAH

HAH

HAH

HOW CAN HE BE THIS FAST?

THIS IS NO ORDINARY MAN.

HAH

COULD HE HAVE...FOUGHT WITH AOSHI-SAMA BEFORE?

HAH

UGYAH!

BTAM

TA

OWWW!

...AUGH! NOW WHERE IS HE?!

!

WE'RE FINISHED...
...PLAYING "IT."

THINK SO, HUH?! WE JUST GOT STARTED!

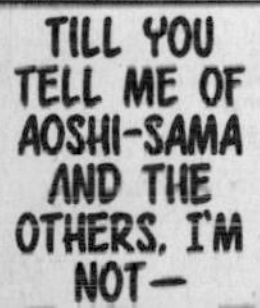
TILL YOU TELL ME OF AOSHI-SAMA AND THE OTHERS, I'M NOT—

ZZ
WHAT...? H-HE COULDN'T HAVE JUMPED THE CLIFF...!
WHAT SHOULD I DO...? I CAN'T JUMP ACROSS—
THEN AGAIN...
HSS
VUPVUP

I HAVE TO STOP HIM.
KANSATSU TOBIKUNAI !!
HE HAS NO CLOAK. AT LEAST ONE WILL HIT, IF I GO FOR HIS LEGS.

THE DAGGERS ...
AH ...
...WITH JUST ONE SWING ...
UH ...
GIVE UP...
...AND GO HOME TO KYOTO.

YOU MAY NEVER SAY HOW AOSHI HAPPENED TO TAKE YOU IN, BUT...
KLEEN
...IF YOU JOIN THE ONIWABANSHŪ, YOU WILL *ALWAYS* BE IN DANGER.

AOSHI MUST HAVE LEFT YOU IN KYOTO BECAUSE HE KNEW THAT.

IT'S BEST TO HARDEN YOUR HEART AND FORGET THEM.
FOR YOUR *OWN* HAPPINESS.

...

TP

TP

TP

SORRY.

WILL YOU QUIT LECTURING ME?!

WHAT DO YOU KNOW?!

"FORGET," YOU SAY!
I'M SEARCHING BECAUSE I *CAN'T* FORGET!!
SHE'S GOING TO JUMP...
—STOP!! YOU CAN'T...
HOW DOES *FORGETTING* THE PERSON I LOVE LEAD TO *HAPPINESS* ...?!

!!!
VM
KH!
GRAB

OOOOOF!!
NO DOUBT ABOUT IT...
...THIS GUY IS GOOD...
SOME-HOW I THINK...
...HE *DID* FIGHT AOSHI-SAMA.
BUT IT'S ALL RIGHT. AOSHI-SAMA WOULD *NEVER* LOSE TO ANYONE.

...

HE'S ALIVE OUT THERE, SOMEWHERE...

...ALONG WITH THE REST OF THE ONIWABANSHŪ.

!

PLIP

HUH... HUH... HUH?!

YOU'RE AWAKE.

VPP

DID I PASS OUT...?

YOU DID.

...NOPE!

I *WILL* SEE AOSHI-SAMA AGAIN, NO MATTER WHAT!!

## The Secret Life of Characters (23)

# —Makimachi Misao—

Kenshin and Kaoru are separated in the current storyline, so I created Misao to serve as the acting heroine.

Because the story's headed in a dark direction, I drew Misao to be as "bright" as possible. It's as though Yahiko + Kaoru / 2 = Misao. Misao's a character I enjoy drawing, and has since become one of my favorites. Plot-wise, she's involved with the Oniwabanshū—an idea that came mainly from reader suggestions about an Oniwabanshū *kunoichi* (female ninja). I'd always planned to use that suggestion in the future... and then it turned out I needed a heroine. To keep the story from becoming more complicated, I decided that a girl who *wouldn't* develop feelings for Kenshin would be a good fit.

Misao will have a painful moment of reunion with Aoshi in the future, but still I want her to keep going strong. A lot of people gave me grief for basing her design on "Nakoruru" in "Samurai Spirits"... but I actually think she's closer to "Mai" or "Yuri" from a certain other battle-game by SNK. (Uh-oh, I'm digging my own grave at the bottom of the grave I just dug!) Guess that cloak I tossed in "just for fun" made a strong impression. As said in Volume 7, I'll try and refrain from doing that too much.

Her design was actually put together pretty quickly. I fussed with the Oniwabanshū ninja outfit a bit, and there it was. In the weekly (*Rurouni Kenshin*) installments, there's already been a minor change—the incorporation of color schemes from the SNK games. What do you think?

Face- and body-wise, Misao was meant to resemble a young man. She's 16, but I wanted her to look more like 13....We argued about the braid in the back, but ultimately decided to keep it, as it added emphasis to her movements.

# Act 65
# Each to His Own Path

THREE DAYS HAVE PASSED SINCE KENSHIN LEFT THE KAMIYA DOJO. HE OUGHT TO HAVE PASSED THE HALFWAY POINT BY NOW, BUT...

HIMURA.

HEY. HIMURA.

IT'S ALREADY NOON.

LET'S EAT SOON.

QUIT IGNORING ME!
!
SHNK

OOOO...
BAH! WHY ARE WE WALKING IN THE FOREST, ANYWAY?!
YOU'RE NOT STILL TRYING TO LOSE ME, ARE YOU?!
THAT HURTS!

THAT'S NOT THE REASON.

IT'S JUST THAT IT'S SHORTER IF WE GO STRAIGHT, RATHER THAN RETURNING TO THE ROAD.

WE SHOULD REACH THE ROAD BY EVENING.
DON'T COUNT ON MUCH REST TILL THEN.

WHY NOT EAT LUNCH WHILE YOU WALK...?
!

ALL RIGHT. I'LL DO THAT.

...HIMURA?
WANT SOME?
ONE MIGHT HAVE BROUGHT BENTO, IF ONE HAD BEEN THINKING.
HARD-TACK
USED TO BE CIRCULAR WAY BACK WHEN.

READ THIS WAY

I WAS...! YOU CAN'T HAVE ANY, THOUGH.
DULY NOTED.
BUT I MIGHT GIVE YOU SOME... IF YOU SPEAK OF AOSHI AND THE OTHERS.
THAT'S QUITE ALL RIGHT.

JUST TELL ME WHAT AOSHI-SAMA AND THE OTHERS...
...ARE DOING RIGHT NOW.

THE OTHERS... THEY...
MEAN-WHILE...
URAH!
BADAM

ORAH!!
URUAH!

HAH
HAH
HAH

THIS IS WRONG.
IT'S JUST DESTRUCTION. NOT TRAINING.

READ THIS WAY

READ THIS WAY

NOTE: DOCTORS PRACTICED MOXIBUSTION BACK THEN

...AS...

URGHAAAH!

...YOU OKAY, YAHIKO?
PRETTY FRICKIN' FAR FROM OKAY...

I NEVER KNEW SHIPS ROCKED SO MUCH...

HOW COME YOU'RE DOING SO GOOD?

WELL, I'M A LITTLE SEASICK...
...BUT I'M NOT ABOUT TO LET THAT STOP ME.

READ THIS WAY

I'VE ALREADY SULKED FOR TWO DAYS... AND WORRIED YOU BOTH.
I'M NOT GOING TO WHINE ANY MORE.
...KAORU GETS HER FEET UNDER HER...
...WHILE YAHIKO DOES QUITE THE OPPOSITE.
UHH—
WAAAARG!
...

NO MORE COMPLAINTS OUT OF ME.
I MUST BE STRONG!

STRONG ENOUGH...
...TO SEE KENSHIN AGAIN...

HAN'NYA-KUN TAUGHT ME HOW TO FIGHT, MATTER OF FACT.

...AND NO ONE'S A GREATER MARTIAL-ARTS MASTER THAN HAN'NYA.

ZK ZK

KSH KSH

OH.

...NOW, I'M ABOUT TO TELL YOU ABOUT AOSHI-SAMA.

AOSHI...

HE'S THE YOUNGEST LEADER OF THE ONIWABANSHŪ EVER! HE'S A GENIUS OF A NINJA...

...A MASTER OF SHORT SWORDS AND MARTIAL ARTS!

Let's talk about the TV anime some more! It may be common knowledge to those of you familiar with manga and anime, but Watsuki actually has very little to do with the anime production (he's too busy with the publishing). Further, due to differences in media, making the manga and anime completely identical would be impossible. As each has its own strength, though, so long as each version takes advantage of those strengths, we're doing okay, right? ...Well, nothing's going to get done with me going on like this. I'll just have to have faith in the professional pride of the anime staff. (That got kind of complicated. Put another way, Watsuki's all for the anime.)

Now, about this game, "Samurai Spirits Zankurō Musōken." I've yet to play it... but I do know "Hisame Shizumaru." Honestly, if the production staff of SNK wants to use "RuroKen" as a model because it's what they think is best for their product, I'm honored. I was pretty down about the letter concerning (my) "Misao" supposedly being influenced by [their game], so after seeing "Hisame," I felt I'd been reprieved. I do have to admit, it was worth a smile! See you next volume.

HE'S RESPONSIBLE, KIND...

...AND THINKS ONLY OF HIS COMRADES.

ON THE OUTSIDE, THOUGH, HE SHOWS NOTHING BUT THE *COURAGE*...

...OF THE ONIWABANSHŪ ONMITSU.

"HE'LL *SMIRK* WITH CONFIDENCE BEFORE A BATTLE TO INTIMIDATE THE ENEMY, OR TO BOOST HIS MEN'S MORALE...

"...BUT HE HAS NEVER *SMILED*."

HE'S PROB-ABLY...
...THE SAME WAY NOW.

READ THIS WAY

...HUH?

YESTERDAY HE RAN THROUGH THE FOREST WITH EASE...

...BUT TODAY ...

HEY.

WHY WASTE TIME PUSHING PLANTS ASIDE?

ISN'T IT EASIER FOR YOU TO WALK THAT WAY?

...I'VE CHANGED MY MIND.
DIG

YOU MUST BE HUNGRY, HIMURA.
YOU CAN HAVE THIS.
ZIP

BUT JUST THE ONE.
THE REST ARE MINE.

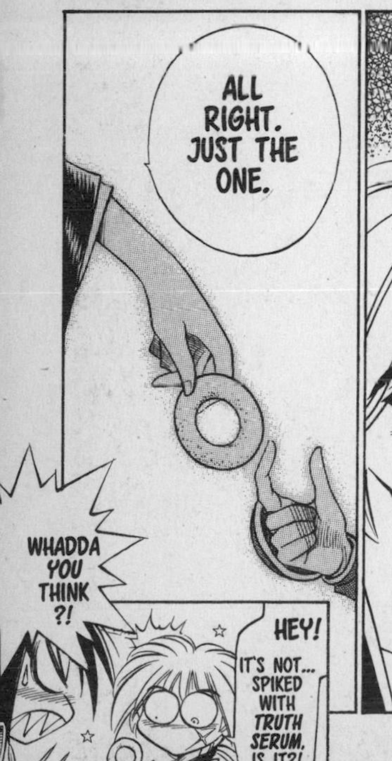
ALL RIGHT. JUST THE ONE.
HEY!
IT'S NOT... SPIKED WITH TRUTH SERUM, IS IT?!
WHADDA YOU THINK ?!

HIMURA, I JUST HEARD A SOUND—
SHH!
STEP AWAY—NOW!—AS *QUIETLY* AS YOU CAN.
SO YOU WEREN'T LYING...
...WHEN YOU SAID SOMEONE'S AFTER YOU?
JUST HURRY.
CURSE IT. IF THEY ATTACK NOW, MISAO-DONO WILL BE INVOLVED.

THERE'S NO CHOICE.
AH...
IT WOULD BE BEST TO STRIKE *FIRST*!!
VSH

HOLD ON A MINUTE!
I *AM* A MEMBER OF THE ONIWABANSHŪ ...!
I CAN BE OF *HELP*-

?!

IS HE... DEAD?
NO...
...BUT...
TM

READ THIS WAY

HAVE YOU ANY LAST WORDS?

!

IT SEEMS THERE'S A *WITNESS* TO YOUR LAST MOMENTS.

ALLOW HIM TO DO WHAT HE CAN.

...P...

...PLEASE...

MY... BROTHER, AND VILLAGE...

SAVE THEM... FROM SHISHIO...

Rurouni
Kenshin

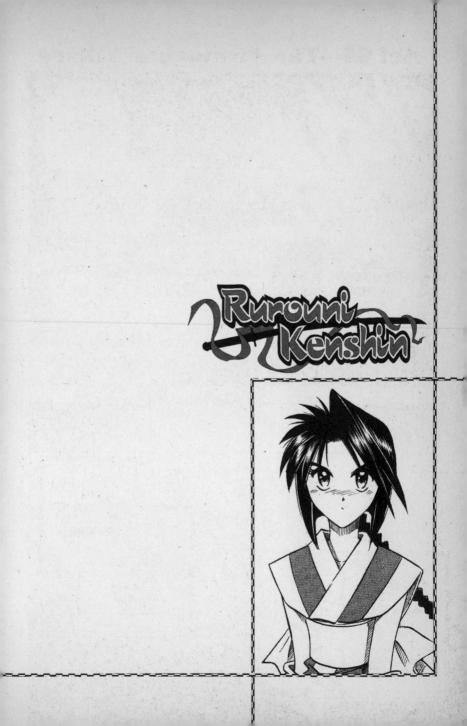

# Act 66—The Abandoned Village

PLEASE...

...SAVE THEM...

...SAVE THEM FROM SHISHIO'S MEN...

THE VILLAGE IS NOT FAR FROM NUMATSU ON THE EAST SEA ROAD...

...ONLY 20 PEOPLE OR SO, HALF FARMLAND AND HALF WOODS.

IT IS CALLED SHINGETSU... "NEW MOON." IT WAS A TYPICAL VILLAGE... UNTIL TWO YEARS AGO.

# Act 66
# The Abandoned Village

SO THIS IS—
WAKE UP.
HEY, WAKE UP!

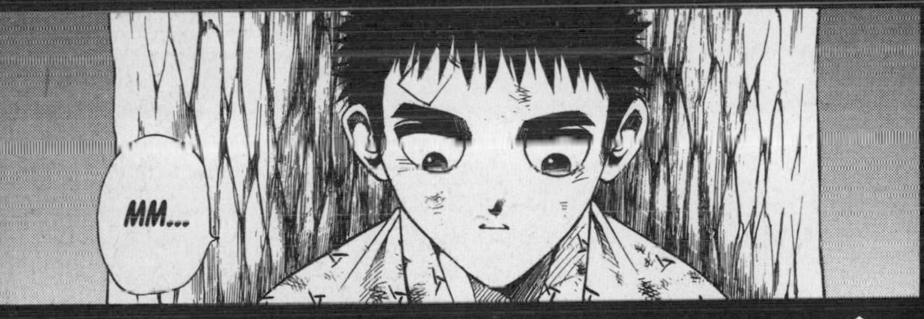
MM...

!
HE'S AWAKE.

YOU... WHAT ...?
WHERE'S MY BROTHER ?!
GASP

WHEN WE FOUND HIM, HE WAS...
CURSE THEM!
PAT
COULD YOU TELL US...
...WHAT'S GOING ON?
WHAT WILL TELLING A STRANGER...
...DO ABOUT IT?
CURSE THEM!

THIS ONE HEADS NOW FOR KYOTO...
...TO CONFRONT SHISHIO.

!!

HSSSSS

TWO YEARS AGO...
...SHISHIO'S HENCHMAN SUDDENLY APPEARED.

HE KILLED THE POLICEMAN STATIONED HERE AND TOOK COMMAND OF THE VILLAGE.
WHEN A *NEW* POLICEMAN CAME, HE KILLED *HIM*.

AFTER TWO YEARS, THE POLICEMEN STOPPED COMING...

...WHILE MORE OF *SHISHIO'S* MEN ARRIVED.

"SHIN-GETSU VILLAGE WAS...

"...ABAN-DONED BY THE GOVERN-MENT."

"ABANDONED" IS A STRONG WORD.

MAYBE THEY'RE PLANNING STRATEGIES.

HSS

THEN WHAT'S THIS?!

FFT

IT'S THE LATEST MAP—BROUGHT BACK BY MY BROTHER FROM TOKYO!

LOOK! SHINGETSU VILLAGE HAS BEEN ERASED!!

BAM!

MY BROTHER SAW WHAT WAS HAPPENING.
HE TRIED TO GET OUR *FAMILY* OUT, AT LEAST...
...AND HE WAS KILLED FOR IT...
...BY THE MAN WHO COMMANDS THIS VILLAGE... A SHISHIO HENCHMAN...
..."SENKAKU," THEY CALL HIM!!

BROTHER...
LEND ME...
GRAB
...YOUR STRENGTH.
IN YOUR BROTHER'S PLACE...
...THIS ONE LENDS YOU HIS OWN STRENGTH.
TP
MISAO-DONO, PLEASE TAKE CARE OF THIS BOY.
WHAT?! BUT I ALSO WANNA—
...NO.
THIS ONE GOES TO THE VILLAGE ALONE.
STAY HERE AND WAIT.
...

THERE'S BEEN NO UPKEEP, NOT FOR A LONG TIME...
IT IS LIKE A GHOST TOWN...

SHISHIO COMES TO THE VILLAGE FOR ABOUT A WEEK, ONCE EVERY HALF-YEAR.
I'VE NO IDEA WHY. BUT *SENKAKU* OCCUPIES OUR VILLAGE FOR THAT REASON ALONE.

SHISHIO IS STAYING AT THE VILLAGE NOW.

SENKAKU HAS GONE TO THE MANSION TO ENTERTAIN HIM...

...SO NOW WOULD BE A GOOD TIME TO GET MOM AND DAD OUT!

GNG!

...EXECUTION.

LACERATIONS ALL OVER THE BODY... LIKE THAT BOY'S BROTHER. THIS MUST BE THE DOING OF SENKAKU.

MOM!
DAD!

READ THIS WAY
!

...YOU.
YOU ARE NOT FROM HERE.

STRANGERS WILL NOT BE LEFT ALIVE!
JAB

WHY DID YOU KILL THESE PEOPLE?

THEIR SONS PLOTTED TO ESCAPE THE VILLAGE.
THEY WERE EXECUTED BY LORD SENKAKU FOR THE CRIME...

...ALTHOUGH WE STRUNG THEM UP AFTER.
STRUNG THEM UP...
...AS AN EXAMPLE.
HEH

LORD SHISHIO *TOOK* THIS VILLAGE FROM THE SWINISH GOVERNMENT!

SHISHIO-SAMA AND SENKAKU-SAMA HOLD THE POWER OF *LIFE* AND DEATH HERE!!

HOH!

AND, BY SENKAKU-SAMA'S ORDERS...

...INTRUDERS MUST DIE!!

!
THUNK
NORMALLY, THIS ONE WOULD SAY, "STEP BACK IF YOU DON'T WANT TO BE HURT."
THIS TIME, THOUGH, IS DIFFERENT.
THIS TIME, EVERY LAST ONE OF YOU GOES DOWN!!
HSS

READ THIS WAY
HEY, GET UP!
HEY!!
I KNOW IT'S HARD...
...BUT THIS IS NO TIME FOR MOURNING!
SHAKE
SHAKE
TM
CRYING WON'T BRING BACK THE DEAD...
...SO STAND UP!!
BY ORDER, INTRUDERS ...
...MUST DIE!
!

YOU!!

WSH

INTRUDERS ...

...MUST D—

!

READ THIS WAY

HMPH.

HYOO

WHO... WHO ARE YOU...?

HUH

THAT IDIOT.

I THOUGHT HE WAS ON HIS WAY TO KYOTO.

WHY IS HE WASTING HIS TIME AROUND HERE?!



**To be continued in Volume 9: Arrival in Kyoto**

# GLOSSARY of the RESTORATION

*A brief guide to select Japanese terms used in* ***Rurouni Kenshin****. Note that, both here and within the story itself, all names are Japanese style—i.e., last or "family" name first, with personal or "given" name following. This is both because* ***Kenshin*** *is a "period" story, as well as to decrease confusion—if we were to take the example of Kenshin's* sakabatô *and "reverse" the format of the historically established assassin-name "Hitokiri Battôsai," for example, it would make little sense to then call him "Battôsai Himura."*

**Himura Kenshin**
Kenshin's "real" name, revealed to Kaoru only at her urging

***Hiten Mitsurugi-ryû***
Kenshin's sword technique, used more for defense than offense. An "ancient style that pits one against many," it requires exceptional speed and agility to master.

***hitokiri***
An assassin. Famous swordsmen of the period were sometimes thus known to adopt "professional" names—***Kawakami Gensai***, for example, was also known as "Hitokiri Gensai"

***Ishin Shishi***
Loyalist or pro-Imperialist ***patriots*** who fought to restore the Emperor to his ancient seat of power

***Kamiya Kasshin-ryû***
Sword-arts or ***kenjutsu*** school established by Kaoru's father, who rejected the ethics of ***Satsujin-ken*** for ***Katsujin-ken***

***Kansatsu Tobikunai***
"Piercing/Killing Flying Daggers"; Misao's special technique

***katana***
Traditional Japanese longsword (curved, single-edge, worn cutting-edge up) of the samurai. Used primarily for slashing; can be wielded either one- or two-handed.

***Bakumatsu***
Final, chaotic days of the Tokugawa regime

***-chan***
Honorific. Can be used either as a diminutive (e.g., with a small child—"Little Hanako or Kentarô"), or with those who are grown, to indicate affection ("My dear...")

***dojo***
Martial arts training hall

***-dono***
Honorific. Even more respectful than ***–san***; the effect in modern-day Japanese conversation would be along the lines of "Milord So-and-So." As used by Kenshin, it indicates both respect and humility.

***Edo***
Capital city of the ***Tokugawa Bakufu***; renamed ***Tokyo*** ("Eastern Capital") after the Meiji Restoration

***Gatotsu***
The signature attack of Saitô Hajime, series creator Watsuki reportedly based his (fictional) version on an actual, historical, horizontal (or "flat") sword-technique.

**Himura Battôsai**
Swordsman of legendary skills and former assassin (***hitokiri***) of the ***Ishin Shishi***

***sakabatô***
Reversed-edge sword (the dull edge on the side the sharp should be, and vice versa); carried by Kenshin as a symbol of his resolution never to kill again

***-san***
Honorific. Carries the meaning of "Mr.," "Ms.," "Miss," etc., but used more extensively in Japanese than its English equivalent (note that even an enemy may be addressed as "***-san***")

***Satsujin-ken***
"Swords that give death"; a style of swordsmanship rejected by Kaoru's father

***Shinsengumi***
"True to the old ways and risking their lives to preserve the old shôgunate system," the popular view of the Shinsengumi ("newly elected group") was that of swordsmen as charismatic as they were skilled. Of note. Thanks to the popularity of the NHK drama of the same name, several historical sites in Japan are reportedly enjoying record attendance levels of late.

***shôgun***
Feudal military ruler of Japan

***shôgunate***
See ***Tokugawa Bakufu***

***Tokugawa Bakufu***
Military feudal government which dominated Japan from 1603 to 1867

***Tokyo***
The renaming of "***Edo***" to "***Tokyo***" is a marker of the start of the ***Meiji Restoration***

***Wolves of Mibu***
Nickname for the ***Shinsengumi***, so called because of the town (Mibu) where they were first stationed

***Katsujin-ken***
"Swords that give life"; the sword-arts style developed over ten years by Kaoru's father and founding principle of ***Kamiya Kasshin-ryû***

**Kawakami Gensai**
Real-life, historical inspiration for the character of ***Himura Kenshin***

***-kun***
Honorific. Used in the modern day among male students, or those who grew up together, but another usage—the one you're more likely to find in *Rurouni Kenshin*—is the "superior-to-inferior" form, intended as a way to emphasize a difference in status or rank, as well as to indicate familiarity or affection

***kunoichi***
Female ninja. In that they are not referred to as simply "*onmitsu*" (ninja), their special name suggests their relative scarcity

***loyalists***
Those who supported the return of the Emperor to power; ***Ishin Shishi***

***Meiji Restoration***
1853-1868; culminated in the collapse of the ***Tokugawa Bakufu*** and the restoration of imperial rule. So called after Emperor Meiji, whose chosen name was written with the characters for "culture and enlightenment"

***patriots***
Another term for ***Ishin Shishi***... and when used by Sano, not a flattering one

***rurouni***
Wanderer, vagabond

# IN THE NEXT VOLUME...

Kenshin arrives in Kyoto and meets Shishio Makoto at last. Although the epic battle between them will have to wait, a glimpse of what lies in store for the new Japan should Shishio's mad ambitions come to pass is revealed. Kenshin's reversed-blade *sakabatô* broken, the question arises: Can it be reforged? *Should* it be reforged? Although Kenshin has abandoned the ways of the *hitokiri*, a new assassin has already taken his place—an assassin whose taste for blood and thirst for power is far greater than ever that of Kenshin....

**On Sale December 2004**
**Now available monthly!**

Ichigo's next opponent is...
his own mother?!
BLEACH
ブリーチ
only $7.95 Each!
Vol. 1-3
Available
Now!
SHONEN JUMP
GRAPHIC NOVELS
on sale now at
www.shonenjump.com
Also available at your local
bookstore, comic store and
Suncoast Motion Picture Company.
COMIC SHOP LOCATOR SERVICE
888-COMIC-BOOK
888-266-4226
BLEACH © 2001 by TITE KUBO / SHUEISHA Inc.
COVER ART SUBJECT TO CHANGE.

THAT DIET BACK IN VOLUME 3? A FAILURE. THIS YEAR, THOUGH, FOR SURE!
YEAH, YEAH.

和月伸宏

NOBUHIRO WATSUKI

## STUFF THAT'S GOT ME DOWN LATELY

SAMURAI SPIRITS: "ZANKURŌ MUSŌKEN" (I WANNA PLAY IT). THE CAFE I GO TO (IT MAY GO OUT OF BUSINESS). DECLINE IN THE QUALITY OF THE PAPER AND PENS WE USE (VERY SERIOUS). MY LOVE HANDLES (EVEN MORE SERIOUS). HOW THE "RUROKEN" ANIMATION WILL TURN OUT (ANTICIPATION). THE DIRECTION THE "RUROKEN" MANGA IS HEADED (SUSPENSE). THE DIRECTION THE MANGA ARTIST "WATSUKI NOBUHIRO" IS HEADED (...).

HERE'S HOPING NEXT YEAR TURNS OUT JUST AS WELL...

***Rurouni Kenshin***, which has found fans not only in Japan but around the world, first made its appearance in 1992, as an original short story in ***Weekly Shonen Jump Special***. Later rewritten and published as a regular, continuing ***Jump*** series in 1994, ***Rurouni Kenshin*** ended serialization in 1999 but continued in popularity, as evidenced by the 2000 publication of ***Yahiko no Sakabatô*** ("Yahiko's Reversed-Edge Sword") in ***Weekly Shonen Jump***. His most current work, ***Busô Renkin*** ("Armored Alchemist"), began publication in June 2003, also in ***Jump***.

**RUROUNI KENSHIN**
VOL. 8: ON THE EAST SEA ROAD
**The SHONEN JUMP Graphic Novel Edition**

STORY AND ART BY
**NOBUHIRO WATSUKI**

English Adaptation/Gerard Jones
Translation/Kenichiro Yagi
Touch-Up Art & Lettering/Steve Dutro
Cover & Graphics Design/Sean Lee
Editor/Avery Gotoh

Supervising Editor/Kit Fox
Managing Editor/Elizabeth Kawasaki
Director of Production/Nobi Watanabe
Editorial Director/Alvin Lu
Executive Vice President & Editor-in-Chief/Hyoe Narita
Sr. Director of Licensing & Acquisitions/Rika Inouye
Vice President of Sales & Marketing/Liza Coppola
Vice President of Strategic Development/Yumi Hoashi
Publisher/Seiji Horibuchi



Printed in the U.S.A.

Published by VIZ, LLC
P.O. Box 77010 • San Francisco, CA 94107

SHONEN JUMP Graphic Novel Edition
10 9 8 7 6 5 4 3 2 1
First printing, October 2004

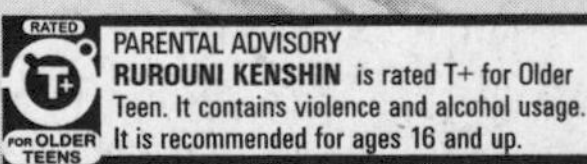